# Mastering the Art

# of Artificial Intelligence:

# A Comprehensive

# Guide

# Book Chapters:

- 

- 

- 

- 

- 

-

- 

- 

- 

- 

- 

- 

- 

**Book Introduction:**

Artificial Intelligence (AI) has emerged as one of the most transformative technologies of our time. From self-driving cars to virtual personal assistants, AI is all around us, shaping our lives in ways we could have only dreamed of a few decades ago. In "Mastering the Art of Artificial Intelligence: A Comprehensive Guide," we embark on a journey to demystify the world of AI and empower you with the knowledge to not only understand AI but also harness its potential.

This comprehensive guide is designed for both beginners and enthusiasts seeking a deeper understanding of AI. We'll start with the fundamentals, exploring the history and evolution of AI, before delving into the core concepts of machine learning, deep learning, natural language processing, and computer vision. Each chapter builds upon the previous one, providing a logical progression that makes even complex topics accessible.

But mastering AI is not just about algorithms and models; it's about ethical considerations and responsible development. In this book, we'll address the critical issue of AI ethics and guide you on the path to building AI models that are both powerful and responsible.

As we journey through these pages, you'll discover real-world applications of AI in healthcare, finance, education, and beyond. You'll learn how AI is reshaping industries and changing the way we live and work. Moreover, you'll gain insights into the future of AI, exploring emerging trends and the challenges that lie ahead.

"Mastering the Art of Artificial Intelligence" is not just a book; it's your passport to the exciting world of AI. Whether you're a student, a professional, or simply curious about the future, this book will equip you with the knowledge and confidence to navigate the AI landscape.

So, fasten your seatbelt, as we embark on this exhilarating journey through the world of artificial intelligence. By the time you reach the final chapter, you'll be well on your way to mastering the art of AI.

# Chapter 1: Introduction to Artificial Intelligence

Artificial Intelligence, commonly referred to as AI, is at the forefront of technological advancement in the 21st century. This field encompasses a diverse array of technologies, algorithms, and methodologies that aim to imbue machines with human-like intelligence. AI is a multidisciplinary venture that explores the development of systems capable of tasks typically associated with human cognition.

The journey into the realm of AI begins with understanding its foundational principles and historical context.

## The Birth of Artificial Intelligence

The roots of AI can be traced to the mid-20th century, where visionaries in the fields of mathematics and computer science contemplated the potential of creating machines that could emulate human thinking. In 1950, Alan Turing proposed a landmark test, now known as the Turing Test, which became a cornerstone in the dialogue about machine intelligence.

## The Early Years of AI

The 1950s and 1960s marked the birth of AI as a formal discipline. During this period, researchers began developing computer programs capable of tasks such as solving complex mathematical problems and playing chess at a high level. One of the earliest AI programs, named the Logic Theorist, was developed in 1956 and could prove mathematical theorems.

## The AI Winter

The late 1960s and 1970s saw a phenomenon known as the "AI Winter," characterized by reduced funding and diminished interest in AI research. The earlier optimism gave way to skepticism due to challenges in creating systems that could handle uncertainty and common-sense reasoning.

## Resurgence and Modern AI

The 1980s and 1990s witnessed a revival of interest in AI. Expert systems, designed to replicate human expertise in specific domains, became a focal point of AI research. Advances in machine learning and neural networks gained prominence, enabling computers to learn from data and adapt to new information.

## The AI Revolution

The 21st century ushered in an AI revolution, driven by breakthroughs in deep learning. This era has seen AI systems achieve human-level performance in tasks like image recognition and natural language processing. Machine learning algorithms have permeated industries from healthcare to finance, facilitating data analysis and decision-making.

## The Scope of Artificial Intelligence

Artificial Intelligence has expanded its influence across numerous domains:

- **Healthcare**: AI assists in diagnosis, drug discovery, and personalized treatment.

- **Finance**: AI powers automated trading, risk assessment, and fraud detection.

- **Autonomous Vehicles**: Self-driving cars employ AI for navigation and decision-making.

- **Natural Language Processing**: AI enhances voice assistants and language translation.

- **Robotics**: AI drives complex tasks in manufacturing and exploration.

- **Education**: AI enables personalized learning experiences.

- **Entertainment**: AI recommends content tailored to individual preferences.

## The Future of AI

The future of AI holds both promise and challenges. Ethical concerns, algorithmic biases, and responsible AI deployment are paramount. Societal and economic impacts of automation will require thoughtful consideration.

The journey into the world of artificial intelligence is an exciting and transformative one. It invites individuals from diverse backgrounds to shape the future of technology. Whether you're a student, a professional, or simply curious, this book will guide you through the captivating world of AI.

# Chapter 2: The History and Evolution of AI

The history of AI is a tapestry woven with brilliant minds, innovative ideas, and pivotal moments. It's a narrative of humanity's relentless pursuit to breathe life into machines, endowing them with the gift of intelligence. Let's embark on a historical journey through the annals of AI.

## Ancient Roots and Philosophical Beginnings

The roots of AI extend far into antiquity. In the works of ancient philosophers, such as Aristotle and Plato, we find contemplation about the nature of thought and reason. They laid the philosophical foundation upon which AI would later be built.

## Alan Turing and the Turing Test

The modern era of AI dawned in the mid-20th century with the pioneering work of Alan Turing. In 1950, Turing proposed the Turing Test, a landmark concept that ignited discussions about machine intelligence. The test sought to determine if a machine's behaviour could be indistinguishable from that of a human.

## The Dartmouth Workshop and Birth of AI

In 1956, the Dartmouth Workshop, organized by John McCarthy, Marvin Minsky, Nathaniel Rochester, and Claude Shannon, marked the official birth of AI as a field. This workshop convened leading scientists and set the agenda for AI research. It was a time of optimism and audacity as researchers believed that they could create machines capable of human-like reasoning.

## Early Challenges and the Pursuit of "General AI"

The early years of AI research were characterized by ambitious goals, including the pursuit of "General AI," or machines with human-like reasoning abilities. However, challenges soon emerged. AI systems struggled with handling uncertainty, natural language understanding, and common-sense reasoning.

## The AI Winter and Periods of Stagnation

The late 1960s and 1970s saw a downturn in AI research known as the "AI Winter." It was a time when funding dwindled, and enthusiasm waned due to unmet expectations. The field faced criticism for not living up to the hype.

## Expert Systems and Knowledge-Based AI

Despite the challenges, AI research continued. In the 1980s, "expert systems" emerged, representing a new direction in AI. These systems aimed to replicate the decision-making processes of human experts in specific domains. They achieved notable success in fields like medicine and finance.

## The Rise of Machine Learning and Neural Networks

The late 20th century witnessed a resurgence of AI, driven by advances in machine learning. Algorithms that could learn patterns from data became central to AI research. Neural networks, inspired by the human brain's structure, gained prominence and proved to be highly effective in various applications.

## The 21st Century AI Revolution

The 21st century brought an AI revolution, fueled by the availability of vast amounts of data and powerful computing resources. Deep learning, a subset of machine learning, emerged as a game-changer.

It enabled AI systems to excel in image recognition, natural language processing, and more.

## AI in the Modern World

Today, AI is not confined to the realm of research labs. It permeates our daily lives, from voice assistants in our smartphones to recommendation systems that suggest what to watch or buy. AI drives innovations in healthcare, finance, transportation, and countless other industries.

## The Future of AI

As we look ahead, AI's trajectory is filled with promise and challenges. Ethical considerations surrounding AI, including bias, transparency, and accountability, require constant vigilance. The societal and economic impacts of automation demand careful planning and adaptation.

# Chapter 3: Understanding Machine Learning

Machine Learning (ML) is the heartbeat of artificial intelligence, driving its ability to learn, adapt, and make decisions. At its core, ML is a set of algorithms that enable computers to learn patterns from data, improving their performance and decision-making over time. In this chapter, we delve into the essence of ML and its significance in the AI landscape.

## The Foundations of Machine Learning

At the heart of ML lies data and algorithms. These algorithms enable machines to recognize patterns, make predictions, and solve complex problems. The core principles of ML include:

- **Supervised Learning**: In supervised learning, models are trained on labelled data, where the correct answers are provided. They learn to map input data to the correct output, making it suitable for tasks like image classification and speech recognition.

- **Unsupervised Learning**: Unsupervised learning deals with unlabelled data, where the model identifies patterns and structures on its own. It's used in clustering, anomaly detection, and dimensionality reduction.

- **Reinforcement Learning**: Reinforcement learning involves training models to make sequences of decisions in an environment to maximize a reward. This paradigm is prominent in training AI for games, robotics, and autonomous systems.

### The Role of Data

Data is the lifeblood of machine learning. ML models learn from data, generalizing patterns to make predictions on unseen examples. The quality and quantity of data greatly impact the model's performance. The advent of big data and increased data availability have significantly fueled the success of ML.

## Training and Testing

ML models undergo training and testing phases. During training, models learn from historical data, adjusting their parameters to minimize errors. Testing assesses how well the model generalizes to new, unseen data. Techniques such as cross-validation and evaluation metrics help gauge a model's performance.

## Overfitting and Underfitting

Balancing a model's ability to capture patterns without overfitting (fitting noise) or underfitting (oversimplifying) is crucial. Regularization techniques and hyperparameter tuning are used to strike this balance.

## The Advancements in Deep Learning

Deep Learning, a subfield of ML, has garnered immense attention for its ability to handle complex tasks. Neural networks, inspired by the human brain's structure, are the cornerstone of deep learning. They consist of interconnected layers of artificial neurons, each performing computations. Deep learning has revolutionized areas like image recognition, natural language processing, and speech recognition.

## Real-World Applications

Machine learning has infiltrated numerous industries:

- **Healthcare**: ML aids in disease diagnosis, predicting patient outcomes, and drug discovery.

- **Finance**: It powers risk assessment, fraud detection, and algorithmic trading.

- **Marketing**: ML enables personalized marketing campaigns, customer segmentation, and recommendation systems.

- **Autonomous Vehicles**: Self-driving cars rely on ML for perception, decision-making, and navigation.

- **Language Translation**: ML-based models can translate languages in real-time.

- **Content Recommendation**: Streaming platforms use ML to suggest movies, music, and products to users.

## Challenges in Machine Learning

While ML has made remarkable strides, it's not without challenges. Ethical concerns, such as bias in algorithms, raise questions about fairness and accountability. Additionally, the need for large amounts of data can pose privacy and security risks.

## The Future of Machine Learning

Machine learning continues to evolve rapidly. Advancements in areas like reinforcement learning, transfer learning, and explainable AI promise exciting developments. The democratization of ML tools and platforms is also making AI accessible to a broader audience.

# Chapter 4: Deep Learning - Unleashing the Power of Neural Networks

Deep Learning, a subset of machine learning, has emerged as a transformative force in the field of artificial intelligence. At its core are neural networks, complex structures inspired by the human brain. In this chapter, we explore the intricacies of deep learning, its architecture, and its profound impact on AI.

## Neural Networks: The Building Blocks of Deep Learning

At the heart of deep learning are neural networks, which are composed of layers of interconnected nodes, known as neurons. These neurons mimic the human brain's processing capabilities, allowing neural networks to learn and adapt from data. The architecture of a neural network typically consists of:

- **Input Layer**: Where data is fed into the network.

- **Hidden Layers**: Intermediate layers that perform computations and extract features from the input data.

- **Output Layer**: The final layer that produces the network's prediction or output.

# Training Deep Neural Networks

Deep neural networks learn from data through a process called training. During training, the network adjusts its internal parameters, known as weights and biases, to minimize the difference between its predictions and the actual target values. This process is typically performed using optimization techniques like gradient descent.

# Convolutional Neural Networks (CNNs)

CNNs are a type of neural network specifically designed for image-related tasks. They excel at tasks such as image classification, object detection, and facial recognition. CNNs use convolutional layers to automatically learn features from the input image.

# Recurrent Neural Networks (RNNs)

RNNs are suited for sequential data, making them valuable in natural language processing and time series analysis. They possess a memory component that allows them to capture temporal dependencies in data.

# Applications of Deep Learning

Deep learning has revolutionized various fields:

- **Computer Vision**: Deep learning powers image recognition, autonomous vehicles, and facial recognition systems.

- **Natural Language Processing (NLP)**: It has enabled language translation, chatbots, sentiment analysis, and speech recognition.

- **Healthcare**: Deep learning aids in medical image analysis, disease diagnosis, and drug discovery.

- **Finance**: It's used in fraud detection, algorithmic trading, and risk assessment.

- **Entertainment**: Deep learning enhances video game AI, content recommendation, and creative tasks like art generation.

## Challenges and Ethical Considerations

Despite its successes, deep learning faces challenges. It often requires large amounts of data, and complex models can be computationally expensive. Additionally, concerns about ethical issues like bias in algorithms and the transparency of decision-making processes are prevalent.

## The Future of Deep Learning

The future of deep learning holds exciting possibilities. Advancements in areas like transfer learning, reinforcement learning, and generative adversarial networks (GANs) promise to expand the horizons of AI. The development of more efficient and ethical AI systems will also be a central focus.

# Chapter 5: Natural Language Processing - Giving Machines the Gift of Speech

Natural Language Processing (NLP) is a fascinating subfield of artificial intelligence that empowers machines to understand, interpret, and generate human language. From chatbots to language translation, NLP plays a pivotal role in making human-computer interaction more intuitive and accessible. In this chapter, we explore the world of NLP and its remarkable applications.

## The Complexity of Human Language

Human language is incredibly complex, characterized by nuance, context, and ambiguity. NLP seeks to bridge the gap between human communication and machines, enabling computers to process and generate text or speech.

## Fundamental NLP Tasks

NLP encompasses a wide range of tasks, including:

**Text Classification:** Categorizing text into predefined categories, such as spam detection or sentiment analysis.

**Named Entity Recognition (NER):** Identifying and classifying entities, such as names of people, organizations, or locations, in text.

**Machine Translation:** Translating text from one language to another, a task central to tools like Google Translate.

**Sentiment Analysis:** Determining the sentiment or emotional tone of a piece of text, often used in social media monitoring and product reviews.

**Chatbots and Virtual Assistants:** NLP enables chatbots and virtual assistants to understand and respond to natural language queries.

# The Role of Machine Learning in NLP

Machine learning techniques, particularly deep learning, have played a pivotal role in advancing NLP. Neural networks, such as Recurrent Neural Networks (RNNs) and Transformers, have demonstrated remarkable performance in NLP tasks.

# Challenges in NLP

NLP faces several challenges, including:

**Ambiguity:** Words or phrases can have multiple meanings depending on context.

**Lack of Context:** Understanding context and drawing inferences from it is a complex task.

**Multilingualism:** NLP must handle multiple languages and dialects.

**Ethical Considerations:** Bias in language models and the potential for misuse raise ethical concerns.

# Applications of NLP

NLP has diverse applications:

**Virtual Assistants:** Voice-activated virtual assistants like Siri and Alexa use NLP for natural language understanding.

**Translation Services:** Tools like Google Translate rely on NLP for language translation.

**Healthcare:** NLP helps extract valuable insights from medical records and assist in clinical decision-making.

**Content Recommendation:** Streaming platforms use NLP to recommend movies, music, and articles.

**Legal and Compliance:** NLP assists in analyzing legal documents and regulatory compliance.

## Ethical Considerations in NLP

NLP's applications also raise ethical questions. Bias in language models, privacy concerns in voice assistants, and the potential for misinformation are important issues. Ensuring fairness, transparency, and responsible use of NLP technologies is essential.

## The Future of NLP

The future of NLP holds promise. Advancements in pre-trained language models, fine-tuning techniques, and multilingual models will continue to expand NLP's capabilities. Ethical guidelines and regulations will shape the responsible development and deployment of NLP technologies.

# Chapter 6: Computer Vision - Teaching Machines to See

Computer Vision is a transformative field within artificial intelligence that equips machines with the ability to interpret and understand visual information from the world around them. It enables applications ranging from image recognition to autonomous vehicles, revolutionizing industries and enhancing our daily lives. In this chapter, we delve into the fascinating world of Computer Vision.

## The Complexity of Visual Data

Visual data is rich and complex, presenting challenges not encountered in other data types. Understanding images and videos requires machines to perceive shapes, objects, movements, and spatial relationships. Computer Vision aims to replicate human visual perception in machines.

## Fundamental Computer Vision Tasks

Computer Vision encompasses a multitude of tasks, including:

**Image Classification:** Assigning labels or categories to images based on their content.

**Object Detection:** Identifying and locating objects within an image or video stream.

**Image Segmentation:** Dividing an image into segments to identify objects and their boundaries.

**Face Recognition:** Identifying and verifying individuals based on facial features.

**Optical Character Recognition (OCR):** Extracting text from images or scanned documents.

## The Role of Deep Learning in Computer Vision

Deep Learning, particularly Convolutional Neural Networks (CNNs), has spearheaded the progress in Computer Vision. CNNs have demonstrated remarkable capabilities in tasks such as image classification, object detection, and facial recognition. They extract hierarchical features from images, enabling machines to recognize patterns and objects.

## Challenges in Computer Vision

Computer Vision presents unique challenges:

**Variability:** Images can vary in lighting conditions, angles, and appearances.

**Scale:** Objects can appear at different scales within images.

**Real-Time Processing:** Some applications, like autonomous vehicles, require real-time decision-making.

**Ethical Considerations:** Privacy concerns in surveillance and facial recognition technologies raise ethical questions.

## Applications of Computer Vision

Computer Vision has far-reaching applications:

**Autonomous Vehicles:** Self-driving cars use Computer Vision to navigate and detect obstacles.

**Healthcare:** Medical imaging relies on Computer Vision for diagnosing conditions like cancer and analyzing X-rays.

**Retail:** Computer Vision enhances customer experiences through cashierless stores and inventory management.

**Security:** Facial recognition systems enhance security at airports and public spaces.

**Agriculture:** Computer Vision aids in crop monitoring and disease detection.

## Ethical Considerations in Computer Vision

Computer Vision technologies often interact with privacy and security concerns. The use of facial recognition in surveillance, for instance, raises questions about civil liberties. Ensuring ethical use and addressing potential biases are ongoing challenges.

## The Future of Computer Vision

The future of Computer Vision is promising. Advancements in neural network architectures, sensor technologies, and edge computing will continue to broaden its applications. Ethical frameworks and regulations will play a crucial role in shaping the responsible deployment of Computer Vision systems.

# Chapter 7: Reinforcement Learning - The Art of Decision-Making

Reinforcement Learning (RL) is a branch of artificial intelligence that focuses on training agents to make sequences of decisions in dynamic environments. It's the foundation of autonomous systems, robotics, and game-playing AI. In this chapter, we explore the principles of RL and its applications.

## The Essence of Reinforcement Learning

At its core, RL revolves around the concept of learning by interaction. An RL agent interacts with an environment, observes the consequences of its actions, and learns to make decisions that maximize a cumulative reward over time.

## Key Elements of Reinforcement Learning

**Agent:** The learner or decision-maker that interacts with the environment.

**Environment:** The external system with which the agent interacts.

**State:** A representation of the environment at a given time.

**Action:** The set of choices available to the agent at each time step.

**Reward:** A numerical signal that indicates the immediate benefit or penalty of an action.

**Policy:** A strategy or rule that guides the agent's decision-making.

## The Reinforcement Learning Process

The RL process unfolds as follows:

- The agent perceives the current state of the environment.

- It selects an action based on its policy.

- The environment responds by transitioning to a new state and providing a reward.

- The agent uses this feedback to update its policy to make better decisions in the future.

## Exploration vs. Exploitation

One of the fundamental challenges in RL is the exploration-exploitation trade-off. The agent must balance exploring new actions to discover optimal strategies and exploiting known actions to maximize rewards.

## Q-Learning and Deep Q-Networks (DQN)

Q-Learning is a foundational algorithm in RL that helps agents learn optimal policies. Deep Q-Networks (DQN) combine Q-Learning with deep neural networks, enabling agents to handle complex, high-dimensional environments. DQN has achieved remarkable success in game-playing AI.

## Applications of Reinforcement Learning

Reinforcement Learning has found applications in various domains:

**Autonomous Systems:** RL powers self-driving cars, drones, and robotics by enabling them to navigate and make decisions in dynamic environments.

**Game AI:** Game characters and agents learn to play games like chess, Go, and video games through RL techniques.

**Recommendation Systems:** RL personalizes recommendations by learning user preferences and optimizing content delivery.

**Healthcare:** RL assists in optimizing treatment plans, patient scheduling, and resource allocation in healthcare settings.

## Challenges in Reinforcement Learning

**Sample Efficiency:** RL often requires many interactions with the environment to learn effective policies, which can be impractical in some applications.

**Exploration Strategies:** Designing effective exploration strategies remains an ongoing challenge.

**Generalization:** Extending RL algorithms to handle diverse and complex tasks is a focus of research.

**Ethical Considerations:** RL in autonomous systems raises ethical concerns regarding safety and decision-making in critical situations.

## The Future of Reinforcement Learning

The future of RL holds exciting possibilities. Research in areas like meta-learning, transfer learning, and continual learning aims to make RL agents more adaptable and capable of handling a broader range of tasks. Ensuring the responsible use of RL in autonomous systems will be paramount.

# Chapter 8: Generative Adversarial Networks (GANs) - Fostering Creativity in AI

Generative Adversarial Networks (GANs) represent a breakthrough in artificial intelligence, enabling machines to create content, images, and even music that closely resemble human creations. GANs are at the forefront of AI's creative capabilities and have applications in various fields. In this chapter, we delve into the world of GANs and their remarkable potential.

## The Genesis of Generative Adversarial Networks

In 2014, Ian Goodfellow introduced GANs, a novel framework for generative modeling. GANs consist of two neural networks, the generator and the discriminator, engaged in a competitive game.

**Generator:** The generator creates data, such as images or text, from random noise.

**Discriminator:** The discriminator evaluates the generated data, attempting to distinguish it from real data.

## The Adversarial Training Process

GANs operate on a simple principle: the generator strives to produce data that is indistinguishable from real data, while the discriminator aims to get better at distinguishing real from fake. This adversarial training process results in the refinement of both networks.

## Applications of GANs

Generative Adversarial Networks have diverse applications:

**Image Generation:** GANs can generate realistic images of objects, faces, or scenes.

**Style Transfer:** They can transform images in various artistic styles, creating impressive visual effects.

**Super-Resolution:** GANs enhance image quality by generating high-resolution details.

**Text-to-Image Synthesis:** They generate images from textual descriptions.

**Deepfake Technology:** GANs can create convincing deepfake videos and audio recordings.

**Drug Discovery:** GANs assist in generating molecular structures for drug discovery.

## Challenges and Ethical Considerations

The power of GANs also raises significant challenges:

**Bias and Misuse:** GANs can amplify biases present in training data and may be misused for fraudulent purposes.

**Deepfakes:** The creation of deepfake content raises ethical concerns related to misinformation and privacy.

**Fairness and Accountability:** Ensuring fairness in GAN-generated content and accountability for misuse is an ongoing challenge.

## The Future of GANs

The future of GANs holds promise and challenges. Research in GAN architectures, such as Conditional GANs (CGANs) and Progressive GANs, aims to improve their capabilities. Ensuring responsible development and deployment of GANs will be crucial.

# Chapter 9: Building AI Models - Tools and Frameworks

In the dynamic world of artificial intelligence, building robust AI models relies on a suite of tools and frameworks that empower developers and data scientists to create, train, and deploy AI solutions. In this chapter, we explore the essential tools and frameworks that underpin AI model development.

## AI Model Development Workflow

Before diving into the tools and frameworks, it's essential to understand the typical workflow for developing AI models:

**Data Collection and Preprocessing:** This phase involves gathering and cleaning data, which serves as the foundation of any AI model. It's crucial to have high-quality, well-organized data.

**Feature Engineering: I**n this step, data is transformed into a format suitable for machine learning. Feature selection and engineering play a vital role in model performance.

**Model Selection:** Choosing the right algorithm or architecture for your AI task is essential. The choice depends on the problem type, data, and desired outcomes.

**Training and Validation:** During this phase, the model is trained on the training data and validated on a separate dataset to assess its performance.

**Hyperparameter Tuning:** Fine-tuning the model's hyperparameters helps optimize its performance.

**Evaluation and Testing:** The model's performance is rigorously evaluated using testing data to ensure it generalizes well to unseen examples.

**Deployment:** Once the model meets the desired performance criteria, it can be deployed to production environments for real-world use.

# AI Tools and Frameworks

Numerous tools and frameworks cater to different stages of the AI model development workflow:

**TensorFlow:** Developed by Google, TensorFlow is an open-source machine learning framework known for its flexibility and scalability. It's widely used for deep learning tasks.

**PyTorch:** Created by Facebook's AI Research lab, PyTorch is a popular deep learning framework known for its dynamic computation graph and user-friendly interface.

**Scikit-Learn:** This Python library offers a wide range of tools for traditional machine learning tasks. It's excellent for data preprocessing, feature selection, and model evaluation.

**Keras:** Keras is an API that runs on top of TensorFlow and other deep learning frameworks. It simplifies the process of building and training neural networks.

**Jupyter Notebook:** Jupyter provides an interactive environment for data exploration, model development, and documentation.

**Pandas:** This library is widely used for data manipulation and analysis in Python.

**Matplotlib and Seaborn:** These libraries are essential for data visualization.

# Cloud AI Services

Major cloud providers offer AI services and platforms that simplify AI model development and deployment, including:

**Google Cloud AI:** Provides tools for machine learning, natural language processing, and computer vision.

**AWS AI Services:** Offers a suite of AI services for speech recognition, image analysis, and more.

**Azure AI:** Microsoft's cloud AI platform offers a range of services for building, training, and deploying AI models.

## Challenges and Considerations

While these tools and frameworks streamline AI model development, challenges include:

**Data Quality:** Ensuring high-quality, clean data is crucial for model success.

Hardware Requirements: **Deep learning models often require powerful** GPUs, which can be expensive.

**Model Interpretability:** Understanding and explaining complex AI models is an ongoing challenge.

**Ethical Considerations:** AI model development should adhere to ethical guidelines, addressing issues like bias and fairness.

# Chapter 12: Real-World Applications of AI

Artificial Intelligence has transcended the realm of theory and experimentation to become an integral part of our daily lives. This chapter explores the diverse and impactful real-world applications of AI across various domains and industries.

## 1. Healthcare

AI has ushered in a healthcare revolution:

**Disease Diagnosis:** AI models excel at analyzing medical images for early detection of diseases like cancer, saving lives through early intervention.

**Drug Discovery:** AI accelerates drug discovery by analyzing vast datasets to identify potential candidates, reducing development time.

**Personalized Medicine:** AI tailors treatment plans based on patient data, improving outcomes and minimizing side effects.

## 2. Finance

In the financial sector, AI has transformed operations:

**Algorithmic Trading:** AI-powered algorithms execute trades with high speed and accuracy.

**Fraud Detection:** AI detects fraudulent transactions by analyzing patterns and anomalies.

**Credit Scoring:** AI models assess credit risk, aiding in loan approvals.

## 3. Retail

AI enhances the retail experience:

**Recommendation Systems:** AI suggests products to users based on their preferences and behavior.

**Inventory Management:** AI optimizes inventory levels, reducing costs and preventing stockouts.

**Visual Search:** AI enables customers to search for products using images.

# 4. Autonomous Vehicles

AI is the driving force behind self-driving cars:

**Navigation:** AI processes sensor data to enable safe and efficient navigation.

**Collision Avoidance:** AI systems detect and respond to obstacles in real-time.

# 5. Natural Language Processing

NLP is pervasive in our digital interactions:

**Chatbots:** AI-powered chatbots handle customer queries and provide support.

**Language Translation:** NLP models translate languages in real-time.

**Sentiment Analysis:** AI gauges public sentiment on social media and news.

# 6. Entertainment

AI enhances the entertainment industry:

**Video Games:** AI creates dynamic and intelligent in-game characters.

**Content Recommendation:** Streaming platforms use AI to suggest movies, music, and shows.

**Content Creation:** AI generates art, music, and even written content.

# 7. Manufacturing

AI optimizes manufacturing processes:

**Quality Control:** AI identifies defects in real-time, reducing waste.

**Predictive Maintenance:** AI forecasts machine failures, minimizing downtime.

# 8. Agriculture

AI modernizes agriculture:

**Crop Monitoring:** AI analyzes satellite and drone data to monitor crop health.

**Precision Farming:** AI optimizes resource usage, reducing costs and environmental impact.

# 9. Energy

AI improves energy efficiency:

**Grid Management:** AI optimizes energy distribution and consumption.

**Predictive Analytics:** AI forecasts energy demand, aiding in resource planning.

# 10. Space Exploration

AI assists in space research:

**Autonomous Rovers:** AI enables autonomous exploration of distant planets.

**Data Analysis:** AI processes and analyzes vast amounts of astronomical data.

## Challenges and Considerations

While AI brings significant benefits, it also raises challenges:

**Ethical Concerns:** AI must adhere to ethical guidelines, addressing bias, fairness, and privacy.

**Data Security:** Protecting data and AI systems from cyber threats is crucial.

**Regulation:** Governments and industries are developing regulations to ensure responsible AI use.

## The Future of AI Applications

The future promises even more exciting AI applications, from healthcare breakthroughs to sustainable energy solutions. As AI continues to evolve, its positive impact on society will grow, making it an indispensable part of our modern world.

# Chapter 13: AI in Healthcare

Artificial Intelligence has emerged as a transformative force in the field of healthcare, offering innovative solutions that enhance patient care, diagnostics, drug discovery, and more. In this chapter, we explore the profound impact of AI in healthcare and its potential to revolutionize the industry.

# 1. Disease Diagnosis and Medical Imaging

AI has revolutionized medical imaging and disease diagnosis:

**Radiology:** AI algorithms analyze X-rays, MRIs, and CT scans, assisting radiologists in detecting anomalies and diseases like cancer, fractures, and neurological disorders.

**Pathology:** AI aids pathologists in the analysis of tissue samples, improving accuracy and speeding up diagnosis.

# 2. Drug Discovery and Development

AI accelerates drug discovery:

**Drug Candidate Identification:** AI analyzes vast datasets to identify potential drug candidates, reducing development time and costs.

**Clinical Trial Optimization:** AI optimizes clinical trial designs, identifying suitable patient cohorts and predicting trial outcomes.

# 3. Personalized Medicine

AI tailors treatment plans to individual patients:

**Genomic Analysis:** AI analyzes genetic data to predict disease risks and optimize treatment.

**Treatment Recommendations:** AI suggests personalized treatment plans based on patient data, improving outcomes and minimizing side effects.

# 4. Telemedicine and Remote Monitoring

AI-powered telemedicine platforms and remote monitoring devices offer accessible and efficient healthcare:

**Telehealth:** Patients can consult with healthcare providers remotely, improving access to care, especially in rural areas.

**Continuous Monitoring:** AI-driven devices continuously collect and analyze patient data, enabling early intervention in cases of deteriorating health.

# 5. Natural Language Processing (NLP) in Healthcare

NLP in healthcare streamlines processes:

**Clinical Documentation:** AI-powered NLP systems transcribe and extract information from patient notes, reducing administrative burdens on healthcare professionals.

**Health Records Management:** NLP helps manage electronic health records more efficiently.

# 6. Drug Adverse Event Monitoring

AI monitors and reports adverse events related to drugs and medical devices, enhancing patient safety and regulatory compliance.

# 7. Predictive Analytics and Early Warning Systems

AI predicts patient outcomes and identifies high-risk individuals, allowing healthcare providers to intervene proactively.

# 8. Surgical Assistance and Robotics

AI-powered surgical robots assist surgeons in performing complex procedures with precision and minimal invasiveness.

# Challenges and Considerations

Despite its immense potential, AI in healthcare presents challenges:

**Data Privacy and Security:** Protecting patient data is paramount, and AI systems must comply with strict privacy regulations.

**Ethical Concerns:** Ensuring that AI is used ethically, addressing bias and fairness issues, is an ongoing challenge.

**Regulatory Compliance:** AI healthcare solutions must meet regulatory standards to ensure patient safety.

# The Future of AI in Healthcare

The future of AI in healthcare is promising. Advancements in AI-driven drug discovery, genomics, and predictive analytics will continue to transform the industry. AI will play a pivotal role in global health initiatives, disease surveillance, and pandemic preparedness.

# Chapter 14: AI in Business: Boosting Efficiency and Profitability

Artificial Intelligence (AI) is revolutionizing the business landscape by providing organizations with powerful tools to enhance efficiency, streamline operations, and increase profitability. In this chapter, we explore how AI is transforming various aspects of business operations.

## 1. Data-Driven Decision Making

AI enables data-driven decision making:

**Data Analysis:** AI systems process vast amounts of data to extract valuable insights, helping businesses make informed decisions.

**Predictive Analytics:** AI predicts future trends and customer behavior, allowing businesses to proactively respond to changing market dynamics.

## 2. Customer Service and Engagement

AI enhances customer interactions:

**Chatbots:** AI-powered chatbots provide instant customer support and information, improving service availability and efficiency.

**Personalization:** AI analyzes customer data to offer personalized recommendations, boosting customer engagement and satisfaction.

## 3. Supply Chain Optimization

AI streamlines supply chain operations:

**Demand Forecasting:** AI predicts product demand, helping businesses optimize inventory levels and reduce carrying costs.

**Logistics and Routing:** AI optimizes shipping routes and delivery schedules, reducing transportation costs and improving efficiency.

# 4. Marketing and Advertising

AI revolutionizes marketing strategies:

**Targeted Advertising:** AI analyzes customer data to target ads to specific audiences, improving ad efficiency.

**Content Generation:** AI generates content, including social media posts and articles, saving time and resources.

# 5. Fraud Detection and Security

AI enhances fraud detection and cybersecurity:

**Anomaly Detection:** AI algorithms identify unusual patterns that may indicate fraudulent activities.

**Network Security:** AI continuously monitors networks for potential threats and vulnerabilities.

# 6. Human Resources and Recruitment

AI streamlines HR processes:

**Resume Screening:** AI automates resume screening and shortlisting of candidates, saving time for HR professionals.

**Employee Engagement:** AI analyzes employee feedback to improve workplace satisfaction and retention.

# 7. Financial Services

AI is transforming the financial sector:

**Algorithmic Trading:** AI algorithms execute trades with precision and speed.

**Risk Assessment:** AI assesses credit risk and investment opportunities with accuracy.

# Challenges and Considerations

Despite its significant benefits, AI in business presents challenges:

**Data Privacy:** Businesses must handle customer and proprietary data with care to ensure compliance with privacy regulations.

**Ethical Concerns:** Ensuring ethical AI use, avoiding bias in decision-making, and addressing algorithmic transparency are important considerations.

**Integration:** Successfully integrating AI into existing business processes and workflows can be complex.

## The Future of AI in Business

The future of AI in business holds promise. As AI technology evolves, businesses will continue to find innovative ways to leverage it to gain a competitive edge, drive growth, and enhance profitability.

# Chapter 15: AI in Finance: Transforming the Financial Industry

Artificial Intelligence (AI) is reshaping the financial industry by providing powerful tools to enhance decision-making, automate processes, and mitigate risks. This chapter explores how AI is transforming various aspects of the financial sector, from banking and investment to insurance and risk management.

## 1. Algorithmic Trading

AI has revolutionized trading:

**High-Frequency Trading:** AI algorithms execute trades at lightning speed, exploiting market inefficiencies.

**Predictive Analytics:** AI predicts market trends and identifies trading opportunities with high accuracy.

## 2. Risk Assessment and Management

AI improves risk assessment:

**Credit Scoring:** AI models assess credit risk, aiding in loan approvals and reducing default rates.

**Fraud Detection:** AI algorithms detect fraudulent transactions by analyzing patterns and anomalies.

## 3. Customer Service and Personalization

AI enhances customer interactions:

**Chatbots:** AI-powered chatbots provide real-time customer support, reducing response times.

**Personalized Recommendations:** AI analyzes customer data to offer tailored financial products and investment advice.

# 4. Wealth Management

AI transforms wealth management:

**Robo-Advisors:** AI-driven robo-advisors create diversified investment portfolios based on client preferences and risk tolerance.

**Portfolio Optimization:** AI continually optimizes investment portfolios to maximize returns and minimize risks.

# 5. Regulatory Compliance

AI assists in regulatory compliance:

**AML (Anti-Money Laundering) Compliance:** AI analyzes transactions for suspicious activities and helps financial institutions meet AML regulations.

**KYC (Know Your Customer) Verification:** AI automates identity verification processes.

# 6. Insurance Underwriting

AI streamlines insurance underwriting:

**Risk Assessment:** AI assesses policyholder risk and sets appropriate premiums.

**Claims Processing:** AI automates claims processing, reducing administrative overhead.

# Challenges and Considerations

AI in finance presents challenges:

**Data Privacy:** Protecting sensitive financial data is crucial, and AI systems must adhere to strict privacy regulations.

**Ethical Concerns:** Ensuring ethical AI use, avoiding bias in financial decisions, and addressing algorithmic transparency are vital.

**Regulatory Compliance:** Financial institutions must navigate complex regulatory landscapes when implementing AI solutions.

## The Future of AI in Finance

The future of AI in finance is promising. As AI technologies continue to advance, the financial industry will increasingly rely on AI for enhanced decision-making, cost savings, and improved customer experiences.

# Chapter 16: AI in Education: Personalized Learning and Beyond

Artificial Intelligence (AI) is reshaping education, offering innovative solutions that revolutionize teaching, learning, and administrative processes. In this chapter, we explore how AI is transforming various aspects of the education sector, from personalized learning to administrative efficiency.

## 1. Personalized Learning

AI tailors education to individual needs:

**Adaptive Learning Systems:** AI algorithms assess students' strengths and weaknesses, adjusting content and pacing accordingly.

**Customized Study Plans:** AI generates personalized study plans for each student, optimizing their learning experience.

## 2. Intelligent Tutoring Systems

AI acts as a virtual tutor:

**Immediate Feedback:** AI provides real-time feedback and assistance to students, helping them grasp difficult concepts.

**Progress Tracking:** AI monitors student progress and identifies areas requiring improvement.

# 3. Language Learning

AI facilitates language acquisition:

**Speech Recognition:** AI-powered language learning apps provide pronunciation feedback.

**Translation:** AI assists in translating text and speech in real-time, aiding language learners.

# 4. Administrative Efficiency

AI streamlines administrative tasks:

**Student Enrollment:** AI automates student enrollment processes, reducing administrative workload.

**Data Management:** AI manages student records, course scheduling, and resource allocation efficiently.

# 5. Educational Content Creation

AI generates educational content:

**Automated Content Creation:** AI generates textbooks, quizzes, and educational materials, reducing production time and costs.

**Language Translation:** AI translates educational content into multiple languages, expanding accessibility.

# 6. Student Support Services

AI enhances student services:

**Chatbots:** AI-powered chatbots handle student inquiries, providing immediate responses.

**Mental Health Support:** AI-driven platforms offer mental health resources and support for students.

## Challenges and Considerations

AI in education presents challenges:

**Data Privacy:** Safeguarding student data is paramount, and AI systems must adhere to strict privacy regulations.

**Equity and Access:** Ensuring that AI benefits all students, regardless of socio-economic background, is a concern.

**Ethical Concerns:** Addressing ethical issues in AI-driven education, such as bias in algorithms and data security, is essential.

# The Future of AI in Education

The future of AI in education is promising. As AI technologies continue to advance, educational institutions will increasingly rely on AI to create engaging, personalized learning experiences, and to streamline administrative processes.

# Chapter 17: The Future of AI: Trends and Challenges

Artificial Intelligence (AI) has come a long way since its inception, and its future holds both remarkable potential and significant challenges. In this chapter, we explore the evolving landscape of AI, highlighting emerging trends and the obstacles that must be overcome for AI to reach its full potential.

## 1. Continued Advancements in Deep Learning

Deep learning, the foundation of many AI breakthroughs, will continue to advance. Key developments include:

**Architectural Innovation:** New neural network architectures will enable more efficient and powerful AI models.

**Transfer Learning:** Models will become better at transferring knowledge from one domain to another, enhancing their adaptability.

## 2. Ethical AI and Responsible Development

The ethical implications of AI will take center stage:

**Bias Mitigation:** Efforts to reduce bias in AI algorithms will intensify, ensuring fair and equitable outcomes.

**Ethical Guidelines:** Widespread adoption of ethical guidelines will guide AI development and deployment.

## 3. AI in Edge Computing

Edge AI, which processes data locally on devices, will become more prevalent:

**Real-time Processing:** Edge AI will enable faster and more efficient real-time data analysis.

**Privacy and Security:** Local data processing will enhance privacy and security, reducing the need for data transmission to centralized servers.

# 4. AI in Healthcare Advancements

AI will continue to transform healthcare:

**Disease Prediction:** AI will predict disease outbreaks and enable proactive interventions.

**Drug Discovery:** AI will accelerate drug discovery, leading to more rapid development of treatments.

# 5. AI in Education

AI will reshape education in various ways:

**Personalized Learning:** AI-driven personalized learning will become more common.

**Global Accessibility:** AI will facilitate access to education for learners worldwide.

# 6. AI in Automation and Robotics

AI will play a more significant role in automation and robotics:

**Autonomous Vehicles:** AI-powered autonomous vehicles will become safer and more reliable.

**Advanced Robotics:** AI-driven robots will perform complex tasks in manufacturing, healthcare, and more.

## Challenges and Considerations

As AI advances, several challenges must be addressed:

**Ethical Dilemmas:** Balancing the benefits of AI with ethical concerns and unintended consequences is a continuing challenge.

**Data Privacy:** Protecting personal and sensitive data while utilizing AI's capabilities is crucial.

**Regulatory Frameworks:** Developing and implementing effective regulations for AI use and accountability is complex.

**Workforce Impact:** Preparing the workforce for AI-related job changes and upskilling is essential.

## The Future is Collaborative

The future of AI is not solely about technology; it's also about collaboration among researchers, policymakers, and industry leaders. Working together, we can harness AI's potential while ensuring that it benefits humanity.